Bilingual Picture Dictionaries

My First Book of
French Words

by Katy R. Kudela

Translator: Translations.com

apple
la pomme
(pumm)

Capstone press

Mankato, Minnesota

Table of Contents

How to Use This Dictionary

This book is full of useful words in both French and English. The English word appears first, followed by the French word. Look below each French word for help to sound it out. Try reading the words aloud.

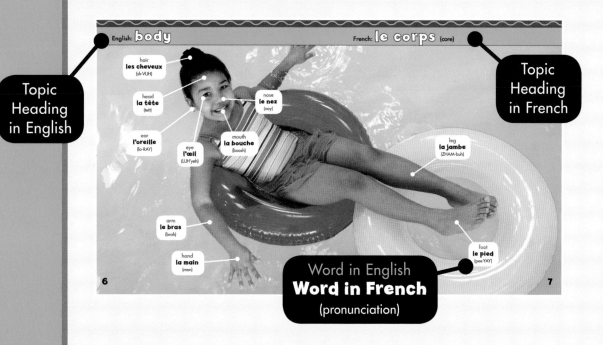

English: **body**   French: **le corps** (core)

hair
les cheveux
(sh-VUH)

head
la tête
(tett)

nose
le nez
(nay)

ear
l'oreille
(lo-RAY)

eye
l'œil
(LUH'yeh)

mouth
la bouche
(boosh)

leg
la jambe
(ZHAM-buh)

arm
le bras
(brah)

hand
la main
(man)

foot
le pied
(pee-YAY)

6   7

Notes about the French Language
The French use the vowel oe. The sound "oe" can change with each word. Look at the pronunciation for help to sound out each word.

The French language usually includes "la," "le," and "les" before nouns. These all mean "the" in French. In French, "du" and "de la" mean some. The pronunciations for these articles are below.

la (lah)   **les** (lay)   **de la** (duh lah)

le (luh)   **du** (dew)

uncle
l'oncle
(LONK-le)

mother
la mère
(mare)

cousin
le cousin
(coo-ZAN)

aunt
la tante
(tahnt)

baby
le bébé
(beh-BEH)

grandmother
la grand-mère
(grahnd-MARE)

father
le père
(pare)

grandfather
le grand-père
(grahnd-PARE)

sister
la sœur
(sur)

brother
le frère
(frare)

5

hair
les cheveux
(sh-VUH)

head
la tête
(tett)

nose
le nez
(nay)

ear
l'oreille
(lo-RAY)

eye
l'œil
(LUH'yeh)

mouth
la bouche
(boosh)

arm
le bras
(brah)

hand
la main
(man)

leg
la jambe
(ZHAM-buh)

foot
le pied
(pee-YAY)

7

pajamas
le pyjama
(pee-zha-MAH)

coat
le manteau
(mahn-TOH)

shorts
le short
(short)

boot
la botte
(bott)

8

shoe
la chaussure
(show-SOOR)

hat
le chapeau
(shah-POH)

pants
le pantalon
(pan-ta-LAWN)

sock
la chaussette
(show-SETT)

dress
la robe
(robe)

shirt
la chemise
(shuh-MEEZ)

kite
le cerf-volant
(sair-voh-LANH)

doll
la poupée
(poo-PAY)

puzzle
le puzzle
(POOZ-el)

train
le train
(trahn)

wagon
le chariot
(shah-ree-OH)

puppet
la marionnette
(ma-ree-oh-NETT)

skateboard
le skateboard
(skayte-BORD)

jump rope
la corde à sauter
(cord a soh-TAY)

ball
le ballon
(ba-LOHN)

bat
la batte
(baht)

picture
le tableau
(tah-BLOH)

lamp
la lampe
(lahmp)

window
la fenêtre
(fuh-NEH-trah)

dresser
la commode
(kum-MODE)

curtain
le rideau
(ree-DOH)

blanket
la couverture
(koo-ver-TUR)

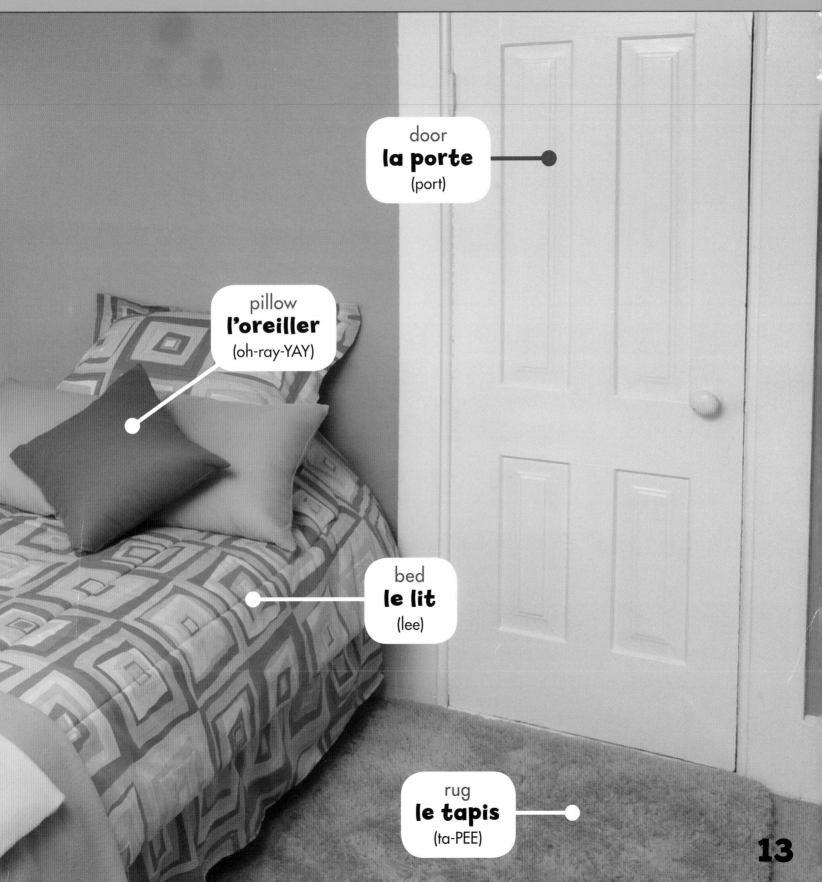

door
la porte
(port)

pillow
l'oreiller
(oh-ray-YAY)

bed
le lit
(lee)

rug
le tapis
(ta-PEE)

bathtub
la baignoire
(bayn-NWAHR)

soap
le savon
(sa-VOHN)

toilet
la toilette
(twa-LETT)

French: **la salle de bains** (sahl duh ban)

mirror
le miroir
(mee-RWAHR)

toothbrush
la brosse à dents
(bross a dahnt)

toothpaste
le dentifrice
(dahn-tee-FREECE)

comb
le peigne
(PAY-nye)

sink
le lavabo
(lah-vah-BOH)

towel
la serviette
(ser-vee-YETT)

brush
la brosse
(bross)

15

pot
la marmite
(mar-MEET)

stove
la cuisinière
(kwee-zee-NYAYR)

bowl
le bol
(bohl)

oven
le four
(foor)

16

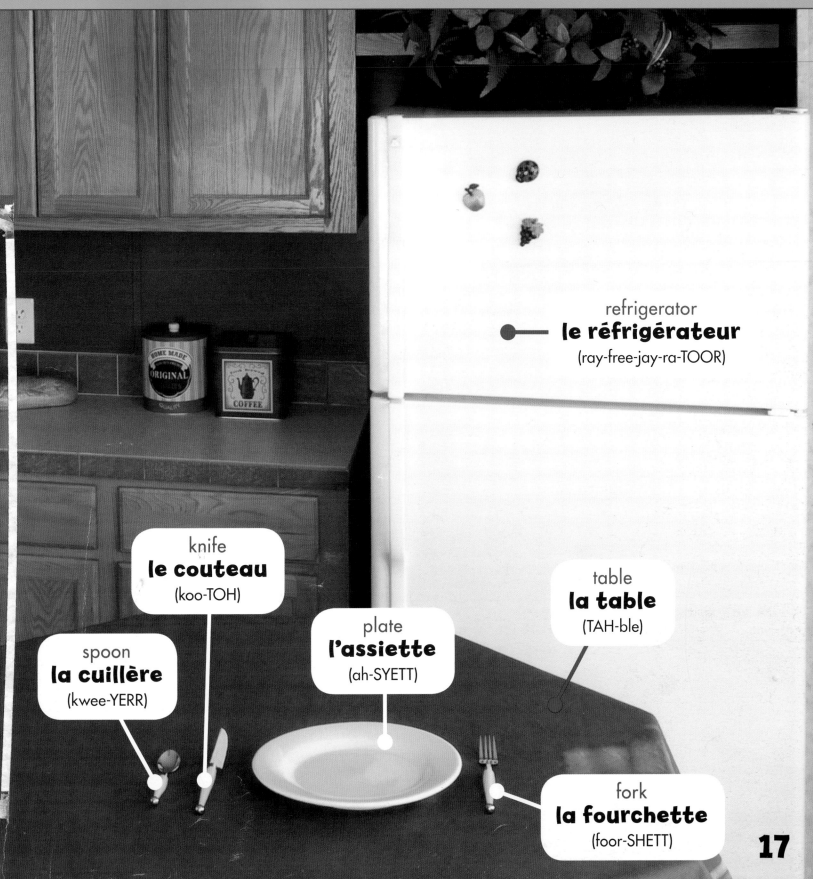

French: **la cuisine** (kwee-ZINE)

refrigerator
le réfrigérateur
(ray-free-jay-ra-TOOR)

knife
le couteau
(koo-TOH)

spoon
la cuillère
(kwee-YERR)

plate
l'assiette
(ah-SYETT)

table
la table
(TAH-ble)

fork
la fourchette
(foor-SHETT)

17

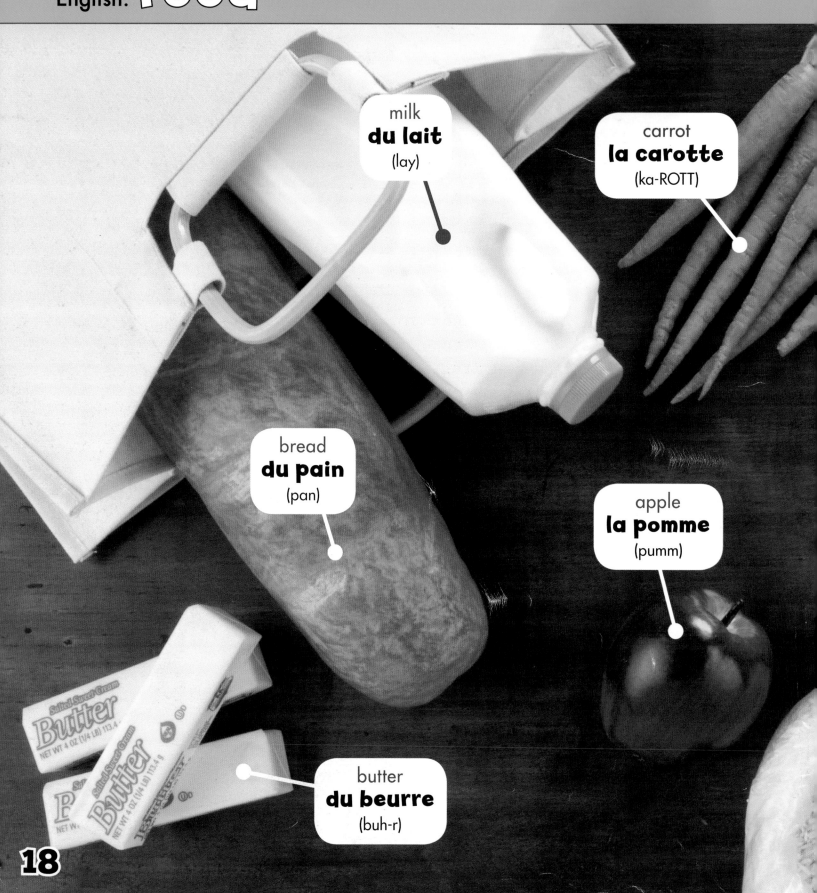

milk
du lait
(lay)

carrot
la carotte
(ka-ROTT)

bread
du pain
(pan)

apple
la pomme
(pumm)

butter
du beurre
(buh-r)

egg
l'œuf
(uff)

pea
le pois
(pwa)

orange
l'orange
(o-RAHNZHE)

sandwich
le sandwich
(sahnd-WEECH)

rice
du riz
(ree)

19

tractor
le tracteur
(trak-TOOR)

hay
du foin
(fwahn)

fence
la clôture
(klo-TUR)

farmer
l'agriculteur
(ag-ree-kool-TOOR)

sheep
le mouton
(moo-TONH)

pig
le cochon
(koh-SHON)

horse
le cheval
(sh-VALL)

barn
la grange
(GRAN'zhe)

cow
la vache
(vash)

chicken
le poulet
(poo-LAY)

21

leaf
la feuille
(FEUY-ye)

butterfly
le papillon
(pa-pee-YON)

flower
la fleur
(flur)

shovel
la pelle
(pell)

bird
l'oiseau
(wa-ZOH)

worm
le ver
(ver)

plant
la plante
(plahnt)

grass
l'herbe
(lairb)

dirt
de la terre
(tair)

seed
la graine
(grehnne)

23

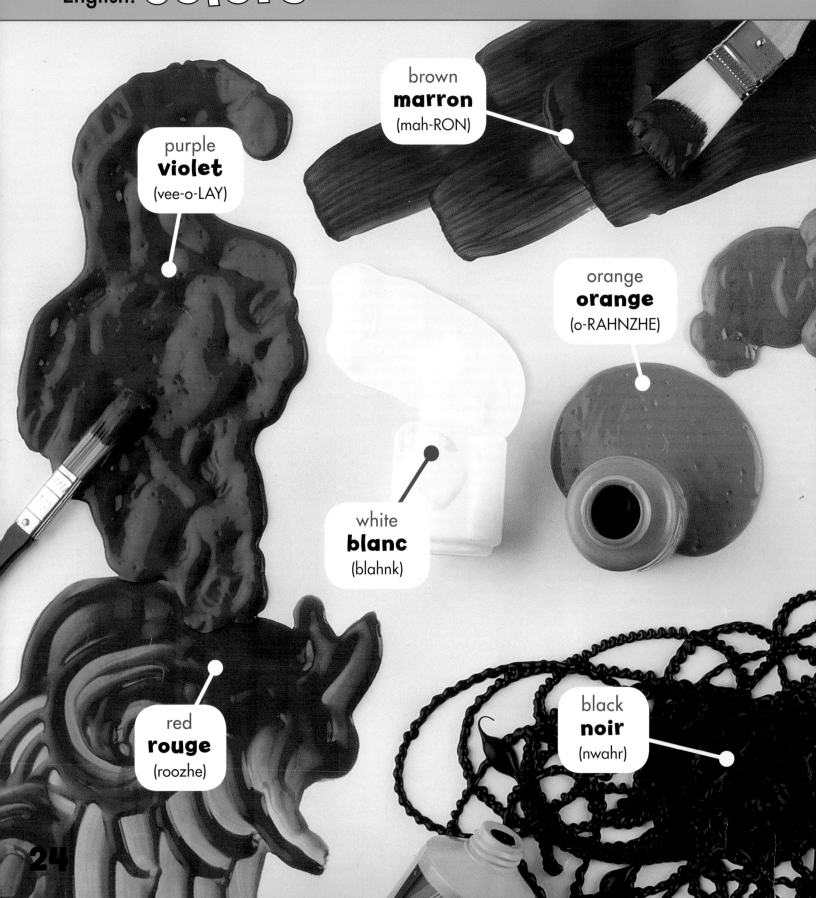

brown
marron
(mah-RON)

purple
violet
(vee-o-LAY)

orange
orange
(o-RAHNZHE)

white
blanc
(blahnk)

red
rouge
(roozhe)

black
noir
(nwahr)

pink
rose
(rohz)

blue
bleu
(bluh)

yellow
jaune
(zhohne)

green
vert
(verr)

teacher
le professeur
(pro-fess-SUR)

book
le livre
(LEE-vrah)

crayon
le pastel
(pahs-TEL)

desk
le bureau
(boo-ROH)

pencil
le crayon
(kray-ON)

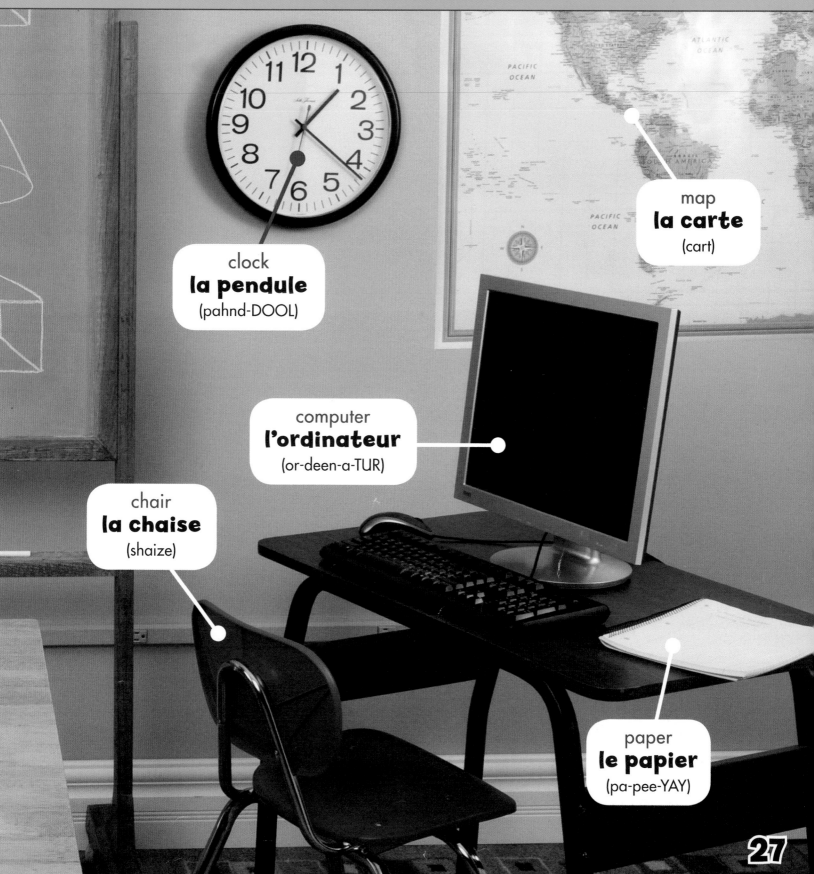

clock
la pendule
(pahnd-DOOL)

map
la carte
(cart)

computer
l'ordinateur
(or-deen-a-TUR)

chair
la chaise
(shaize)

paper
le papier
(pa-pee-YAY)

traffic light
le feu de signalisation
(fuh de see-nyah-lee-za-SEE-OHN)

library
la bibliothèque
(bib-lee-o-TEK)

store
le magasin
(ma-ga-ZAHN)

LIBRARY

ONE WAY

Tuesday 2:00–5:00
Thursday 2:00–6:00

bicycle
le vélo
(vay-LO)

car
la voiture
(vwa-TUR)

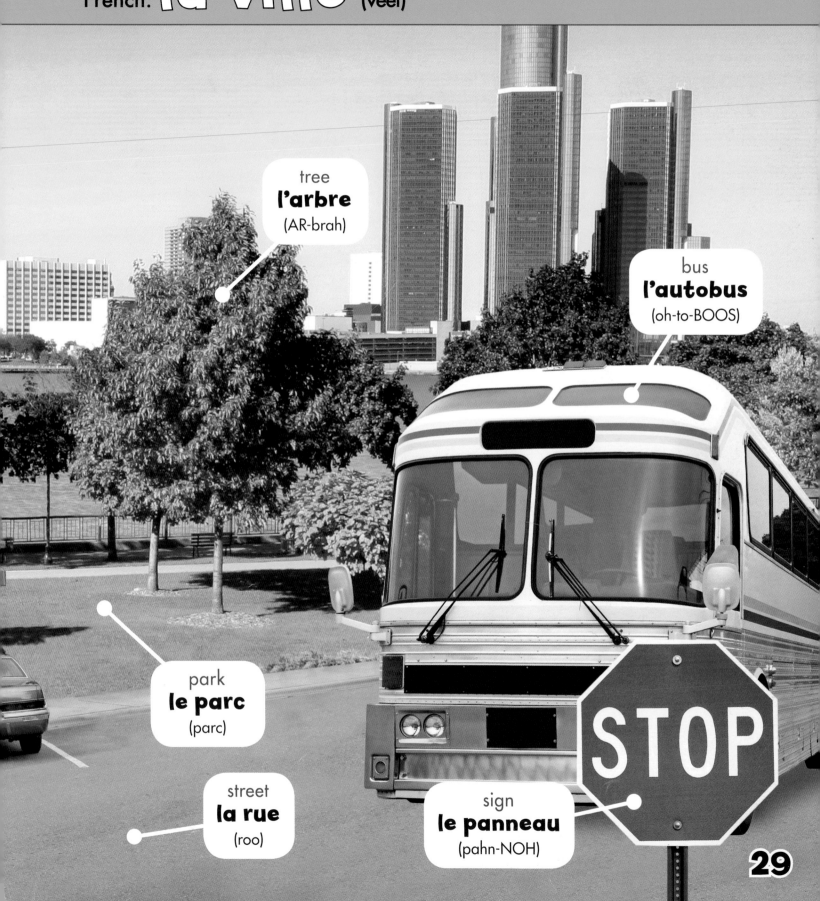

tree
l'arbre
(AR-brah)

bus
l'autobus
(oh-to-BOOS)

park
le parc
(parc)

street
la rue
(roo)

sign
le panneau
(pahn-NOH)

STOP

29

Numbers • Les chiffres (SHEE-freh)

1. one • **un** (un)
2. two • **deux** (duh)
3. three • **trois** (twah)
4. four • **quatre** (KAT-trah)
5. five • **cinq** (sank)

6. six • **six** (seece)
7. seven • **sept** (sett)
8. eight • **huit** (weet)
9. nine • **neuf** (neuff)
10. ten • **dix** (deece)

Useful Phrases • Expressions utiles (ex-press-SYON oo-TEEL)

yes • **oui** (wee)

no • **non** (no'n)

hello • **bonjour** (bone-ZHOOR)

good-bye • **au revoir** (oh ruh-VWAR)

good morning • **bonjour** (bone-ZHOOR)

good night • **bonne nuit** (bunn NWEE)

please • **s'il vous plait** (see voo play)

thank you • **merci** (mer-SEE)

excuse me • **excusez-moi** (ex-KOO-zay-mwa)

My name is _____. • **Mon nom est _____.** (Mohn nawm ay)

Read More

French Picture Dictionary. Princeton, N.J.: Berlitz, 2004.

Stanley, Mandy. *My First French Book*. New York: Kingfisher, 2007.

Vox First French Picture Dictionary. Chicago: McGraw-Hill, 2004.

Internet Sites

FactHound offers a safe, fun way to find Internet sites related to this book. All of the sites on FactHound have been researched by our staff.

Here's all you do:

Visit *www.facthound.com*

FactHound will fetch the best sites for you!

A+ Books are published by Capstone Press,
151 Good Counsel Drive, P.O. Box 669, Mankato, Minnesota 56002.
www.capstonepub.com

022010
005713R

Books published by Capstone Press are manufactured with paper
containing at least 10 percent post-consumer waste.

Library of Congress Cataloging-in-Publication Data
Kudela, Katy R.
   My first book of French words / by Katy R. Kudela.
   p. cm. — (A+ books. Bilingual picture dictionaries)
   Summary: "Simple text paired with themed photos invite the reader to learn to speak
French" — Provided by publisher.
   Includes bibliographical references.
   ISBN 978-1-4296-3295-9 (library binding)
   ISBN 978-1-4296-4369-6 (paperback)
   1. Picture dictionaries, French — Juvenile literature. 2. Picture dictionaries, English —
Juvenile literature. 3. French language — Dictionaries, Juvenile — English.
4. English language — Dictionaries, Juvenile — French. I. Title. II. Series.
PC2629.K83 2010
443'.21 — dc22   2009005510

Credits
Juliette Peters, designer; Wanda Winch, media researcher

Photo Credits
Capstone Press/Gary Sundermeyer, cover (pig), 20 (farmer with tractor, pig)
Capstone Press/Karon Dubke, cover (ball, sock), back cover (toothbrush, apple), 1, 3,
   4–5, 6–7, 8–9, 10–11, 12–13, 14–15, 16–17, 18–19, 22–23, 24–25, 26–27
Image Farm, back cover, 1, 2, 31, 32 (design elements)
iStockphoto/Andrew Gentry, 28 (main street)
Photodisc, cover (flower)
Shutterstock/Adrian Matthiassen, cover (butterfly); David Hughes, 20 (hay); Eric Isselee,
   20–21 (horse); hamurishi, 28 (bike); Jim Mills, 29 (stop sign); Kelli Westfal, 28
   (traffic light); Levgeniia Tikhonova, 21 (chickens); Margo Harrison, 20 (sheep);
   MaxPhoto, 21 (cow and calf); Melinda Fawver, 29 (bus); Robert Elias, 20–21
   (barn, fence); Vladimir Mucibabic, 28–29 (city skyline)

Note to Parents, Teachers, and Librarians
Learning to speak a second language at a young age has been shown to improve overall
academic performance, boost problem-solving ability, and foster an appreciation for other
cultures. Early exposure to language skills provides a strong foundation for other subject
areas, including math and reasoning. Introducing children to a second language can help
to lay the groundwork for future academic success and cultural awareness.